History of the Federal Reserve

AF115414

Table of Contents

1951 Accord 1
Aldrich–Vreeland Act 1
Allan H. Meltzer 2
Federal Reserve Reform Act of 1977 . 2
Federal Reserve responses to the subprime crisis 4
History of Federal Open Market Committee actions 6
History of the Federal Reserve System9
Jekyll Island 14
Paul Warburg 18
Too big to fail.................................. 20
Walter Wyatt 23

Preface

Each chapter in this book ends with a URL to a hyperlinked online version. Use the online version to access related pages, websites, footnotes, tables, color photos, updates, or to see the chapter's contributors. Click the edit link to suggest changes. Please type the URL exactly as it appears. If you change the URL's capitalization, for example, it may not work.

Purchase of this book entitles you to a free trial membership in the publisher's book club at www.booksllc.net. (Time limited offer.) Simply enter the barcode number from the back cover onto the membership form on our home page. The book club entitles you to select from millions of books at no additional charge, including a PDF copy of this and related books to read on the go. Simply enter the title or subject onto the search form to find them.

If you have any questions, could you please be so kind as to consult our Frequently Asked Questions page at www.booksllc.net/faqs.cfm? You are also welcome to contact us there.

Publisher: Books LLC, Wiki Series, Memphis, TN, USA, 2013.

1951 Accord

The **1951 Accord**, also known simply as the **Accord**, was an agreement between the U.S. Department of the Treasury and the Federal Reserve that restored independence to the Fed.

During World War II, the Fed pledged to keep the interest rate on Treasury bills fixed at 0.375 percent. It continued to support government borrowing after the war ended, despite the fact that the Consumer Price Index rose 14% in 1947 and 8% in 1948, and the economy was in recession. President Harry S. Truman in 1948 replaced then Chairman of the Federal Reserve Marriner Eccles with Thomas B. McCabe for opposing this policy, although Eccles's term on the board would continue for three more years. The reluctance of the Fed to continue monetizing the deficit became so great that in 1951, President Truman invited the entire Federal Open Market Committee to the White House to resolve their differences. William McChesney Martin, then Assistant Secretary of the Treasury, was the principal mediator. Three weeks later, he was named Chairman of the Fed, replacing McCabe.

Source http://en.wikipedia.org/wiki/1951_Accord

Aldrich–Vreeland Act

The **Aldrich–Vreeland Act** was passed in response to the Panic of 1907 and established the National Monetary Commission, which recommended the Federal Reserve Act of 1913.

On May 27, 1908, the bill passed the House on a mostly party-line vote of 166–140, with 13 Republicans voting against it and no Democrats voting for it. On May 30, it passed in the Senate with 43 Republicans in favor and five Republicans joining 17 Democrats opposed. President Roosevelt signed the bill that same night.

The act also allowed national banks to start national currency associations in groups of ten or more, with at least $5 million in total capital, to issue emergency currency. These bank notes were not to be backed by just government bonds, but also just about any securities the banks were holding. The act proposed that this emergency currency had to go through a process of approval by the officers of these national currency associations, and then once approved were distributed by the Comptroller of the Currency. However, it is possible that because there was a 5 percent tax placed on this emergency currency for the first month it was "outstanding" and a 1 percent increase for the following months it was "outstanding," no bank notes were issued. Another possible explanation why the emergency currency never issued might have been because it wasn't necessary to do so.

Congress modified and extended the law in 1914 when British and other foreign creditors demanded immediate payments, in gold, of amounts which would ordinarily have been carried over and paid through exports of commodities.

Senator Nelson W. Aldrich (R-RI) was largely responsible for the *Aldrich-Vreeland Currency Law*, and he became the Chairman of the *National Monetary commission*. The co-sponsor of the legislation was Rep. Edward Vreeland, a Republican from New York.

A usage of the law occurred at the outbreak of the World War I in 1914 when the first great financial panic of the 20th century befell the world, necessitating the closure of the New York Stock Exchange. Secretary of the Treasury William Gibbs McAdoo appeared in New York City and assured the public that ample stocks of emergency bank notes had been prepared in accordance with the Aldrich–Vreeland Act and were available for issue to the banks. As of October 23, 1914, $368,616,990 was outstanding.

The Federal Reserve Act of December 23, 1913 took effect in November 1914 when the 12 regional banks opened for business. Ultimately the emergency currency issued under the *Aldrich-Vreeland Law* was entirely withdrawn.

Source http://en.wikipedia.org/wiki/Aldrich–Vreeland_Act

Allan H. Meltzer

Born	February 6, 1928
	Boston, Massachusetts
Nationality	American
Field	Economist
Influences	Milton Friedman

Allan H. Meltzer is an American economist and professor of Political Economy at Carnegie Mellon University's Tepper School of Business in Pittsburgh, Pennsylvania. He was born February 6, 1928, in Boston, Massachusetts. He is the author of dozens of academic papers and books on monetary policy and the Federal Reserve Bank, and is considered one of the world's foremost experts on the development and applications of monetary policy.

Meltzer is currently president of the Mont Pelerin Society for the 2012-2014 term.

Meltzer's study *A History of the Federal Reserve* is considered the most comprehensive history of the central bank. Volume I was released in Novermber 2002; Volume II, which covers the years since the Federal Reserve accord in 1951 to 1969, was released in February, 2010.

Meltzer has confirmed to have originated the aphorism "Capitalism without failure is like religion without sin. It doesn't work."

Career

Meltzer received his A.B. and M.A. degrees from Duke University in 1948 and 1955, respectively. He earned his Ph.D. degree from UCLA in 1958.

Meltzer served, from 1973 to 1999, as the Chair of the Shadow Open Market Committee, a group of economists, academics, and bankers that met to critique the actions of the Federal Reserve's Federal Open Market Committee. He served on the Council of Economic Advisors for both Presidents Kennedy and Ronald Reagan. He is currently a visiting scholar at the American Enterprise Institute.

Meltzer was the Chairman of the International Financial Institution Advisory Commission, known as the Meltzer Commission. The Commission's majority report proposed changes to the operations of the International Monetary Fund and especially to those of the World Bank, which the majority recommended should withdraw from lending to "middle income countries". Four (out of 5) Commission members nominated by the then-minority Congressional Democrats filed a dissent from the majority's recommendations (Bergsten, Huber, Levinson and Torres), though one of the four (Huber) both voted for the majority report and joined the dissent. The official vote tally in favor was thus recorded as 8 to 3. Controversy over the majority's arguments and recommendations continued after the report's publication: the majority's core recommendations are defended by Chairman Meltzer's chief advisor Adam Lerrick, and challenged by one of the Commission's critics (David de Ferranti), in their respective chapters in an edited volume published by the Center for Global Development and fully accessible on the web .

Meltzer was the first ever recipient of the AEI's Irving Kristol award in 2003. He was honored at the award dinner by President George W. Bush, who remarked "I know I'm not the featured speaker; I'm just a warm-up act for Allan Meltzer."

Meltzer was highly critical of the Federal Reserve's September 2008 decision to rescue the leading bond-insurer AIG: "these disasters should be headed off early, or should be left to the marketplace to settle." Consistent with this position, the Fed's decision *not* to rescue Lehman Brothers was one which, at the time, Meltzer appeared to applaud. Contrasting it with the AIG rescue, he commented: "I would say we ought to look at Lehman Brothers. They let Lehman Brothers fail. Within a few days, just a few days, Barclays was there buying up some of Lehman's assets..." A year later, however, Meltzer took a more critical view of the Fed's handling of the Lehman case: "After 30 years of bailing out almost all large financial firms, the Fed made the horrendous mistake of changing its policy in the midst of a recession... Allowing Lehman to fail without warning is one of the worst blunders in Federal Reserve history..."

Meltzer has opposed US adoption of a "cap and trade" scheme for carbon emissions, designed to help combat global climate change.

Source http://en.wikipedia.org/wiki/Allan_H._Meltzer

Federal Reserve Reform Act of 1977

Full title An Act to extend the authority for the flexible regulation of interest rates on deposits and accounts in depository institutions, to promote the accountability of the Federal Reserve System, and for other purposes.

Enacted by the 95th United States Congress

Effective November 16, 1977

Citations

Public Law Pub.L. 95–188

Stat. 91 Stat. 1387

Codification

Federal Reserve Act

Bank Holding Company Act of 1956

Legislative history

Introduced in the House as H.R. 9710 **by** Henry S. Reuss (D–WI) **on** October 20, 1977

Passed the House on October 31, 1977 (395–3)

Passed the Senate on November 1, 1977 () **with amendment**

House agreed to Senate amendment on November 2, 1977 ()

Signed into law by President Jimmy Carter **on** November 16, 1977

The **Federal Reserve Reform Act of 1977** enacted a number of reforms to the Federal Reserve, making it more accountable for its actions on monetary and fiscal policy and tasking it with the goal to "promote maximum employment, production, and price stability". The act explicitly established price stability as a national policy goal for the first time. It also required quarterly reports to Congress "concerning the ranges of monetary and credit aggregrates for the upcoming 12 months." It also modified the selection of the Class B and C Reserve Bank Directors. Discrimination on the basis of race, creed, color, sex, or national origin was prohibited, and the composition of the directors was required to represent interests of "agriculture, commerce, industry, services, labor and consumers". The Federal Reserve Act, which created the Federal Reserve in 1913, made no mention of services, labor, and consumers. Finally, the act established Senate confirmation of chairmen and vice chairmen of the Board of Governors of the Federal Reserve. The Federal Reserve Reform Act made the Federal Reserve more transparent to Congressional oversight.

Historical Context and Objectives

Much of the text of the Federal Reserve Reform Act pertains to Congress leveraging its oversight power over the Federal Reserve to make it disclose its monetary objectives. Since Congressional Resolution 133 was passed in 1975, the Federal Open Market Committee had announced the long-term monetary aggregates of M1, M2, and M3. This policy was codified in the Federal Reserve Reform Act. Congress enacted this policy under the belief that the actions of the Federal Reserve directly impacted the business climate, and it wanted to keep track of the Federal Reserve's attempts to alter it. Leaders at the Federal Reserve who objected were not necessarily motivated by a desire for secrecy. Rather, they felt that disclosing the Fed's views made their plans more difficult to realize in the future, because markets would respond to the Fed's plans and alter the Fed's projections. In other words, certain market actors would use the Fed's disclosures to engage in profitable investments, which would alter market outcomes and neutralize the Federal Reserve's actions. Furthermore, the Federal Reserve argued that this benefit would accrue to a few individuals, which would not be in the public interest. This was the reason that the Fed regularly overshot targets for money growth until the Volcker years.

The Federal Reserve Reform Act of 1977 was passed in short succession with a number of other bills regulating the Federal Reserve. Namely:

Congressional Resolution 133 on March 25, 1975

Full Employment and Balanced Growth Act of 1978

Government in the Sunshine Act, effective on March 12, 1977

Outline of the Reform Act

The Federal Reserve Reform Act of 1977 is composed of three titles:

Title I: Regulation of Interest Rates

Extends the authority of the Board of Governors of the Federal Reserve System to regulate interest rates on deposits and accounts in insured institutions by one year until December 15, 1978.

Title II: Amendments to the Federal Reserve Act

Amends the Federal Reserve Act to require the Board of Governors of the Federal Reserve System and the Federal Open Market Committee to maintain the long-run growth of the monetary and credit aggregates commensurate with the economy's production potential.

Prohibits discrimination in the selection of the Board of Directors of the Federal Reserve System.

Requires Senate confirmation of the Chairman and Vice Chairman of the Board of Governors, effective in 1979. States that such officers will have four-year terms.

Makes it a criminal offense for a Federal Reserve Bank officer, employee, or director to participate in specified activities affecting personal financial interests.

Title III: Amendments to the Bank Holding Company Act of 1956

Amends the Bank Holding Company Act of 1956 to authorize the Board of Governors of the Federal Reserve System upon application of a bank holding company to extend the two-year period during which a company may dispose of shares acquired in the course of securing or collecting a debt.

Permits the waiver of the 30-day notice requirement for acquisitions of banks by holding companies and the immediate consummation of such transaction when the transaction would facilitate the acquisition of a failing bank. Source http://en.wikipedia.org/wiki/Federal_Reserve_Reform_Act_of_1977

Federal Reserve responses to the subprime crisis

The U.S. central banking system, the Federal Reserve, in partnership with central banks around the world, took several steps to address the subprime mortgage crisis. Federal Reserve Chairman Ben Bernanke stated in early 2008: "Broadly, the Federal Reserve's response has followed two tracks: efforts to support market liquidity and functioning and the pursuit of our macroeconomic objectives through monetary policy. A 2011 study by the Government Accountability Office found that "on numerous occasions in 2008 and 2009, the Federal Reserve Board invoked emergency authority under the Federal Reserve Act of 1913 to authorize new broad-based programs and financial assistance to individual institutions to stabilize financial markets. Loans outstanding for the emergency programs peaked at more than $1 trillion in late 2008."

Signaling

In August 2007,Committee announced that "downside risks to growth have increased appreciably," a signal that interest rate cuts might be forthcoming. Between 18 September 2007 and 30 April 2008, the target for the Federal funds rate was lowered from 5.25% to 2% and the discount rate was lowered from 5. 75% to 2.25%, through six separate actions. The discount rate is the interest rate charged to commercial banks and other depository institutions on loans they receive from their regional Federal Reserve Bank's lending facility via the Discount window.

Expansion of Fed Balance Sheet ("Credit easing")

The Fed can electronically create money and use it to lend against collateral of various types, such as agency mortgage-backed securities or asset-backed commercial paper. This is effectively "printing money" and increases the money supply, which under normal economic

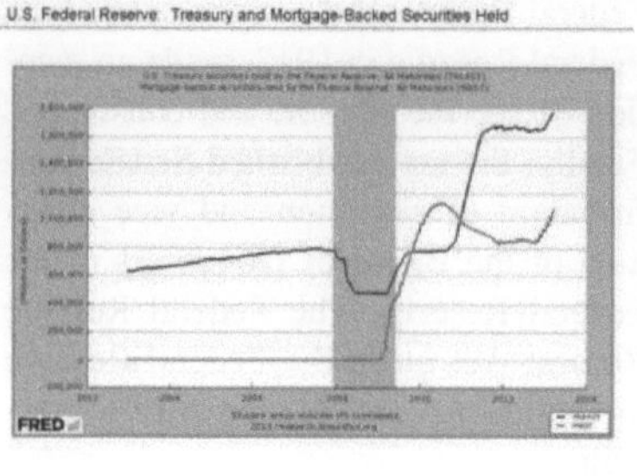

Federal Reserve Holdings of Treasury and Mortgage-Backed Securities

conditions creates inflationary pressure. Ben Bernanke called this approach "credit easing", possibly to distinguish it from the widely used expression Quantitative easing, which however originally also referred to the expansion of "credit creation" (reference: Richard Werner, Keizai Kyoshitsu: Keiki kaifuku, Ryoteiki kinyu kanwa kara, Nikkei, Nihon Keizai Shinbun, 2 September 1995) . In a March 2009 interview, he stated that the expansion of the Fed balance sheet was necessary "...because our economy is very weak and inflation is very low. When the economy begins to recover, that will be the time that we need to unwind those programs, raise interest rates, reduce the money supply, and make sure that we have a recovery that does not involve inflation."

Both the actual and authorized size of the Fed balance sheet (i.e., the amount it is allowed to borrow from the Treasury to lend) was increased significantly during the crisis. The money created was funneled through certain financial institutions, which use it to lend to corporations issuing the financial instruments that serve as collateral. The type or scope of assets eligible to be collateral for such loans has expanded throughout the crisis.

In March 2009, the Federal Open Market Committee (FOMC) decided to increase the size of the Federal Reserve's balance sheet further by purchasing up to an additional $750 billion of government-sponsored agency mortgage-backed securities, bringing its total purchases of these securities to up to $1.25 trillion during 2009, and to increase its purchases of agency debt this year by up to $100 billion to a total of up to $200 billion. Moreover, to help improve conditions in private credit markets, the Committee decided to purchase up to $300 billion of longer-term Treasury securities during 2009.

Mortgage lending rules

In July 2008, the Fed finalized new rules that apply to mortgage lenders. Fed Chairman Ben Bernanke stated that the rules "prohibit lenders from making higher-priced loans without due regard for consumers' ability to make the scheduled payments and require lenders to verify the income and assets on which they rely when making the credit decision. Also, for higher-priced loans, lenders now will be required to establish escrow accounts so that property taxes and insurance costs will be included in consumers' regular monthly payments.. .Other measures address the coercion of appraisers, servicer practices, and other issues. We believe the new rules will help to restore confidence in the mortgage market."

Open market operations

Agency Mortgage-Backed Securities (MBS) Purchase Program

The Fed and other central banks have conducted open market operations to ensure member banks have access to funds (i.e., liquidity). These are effectively short-term loans to member banks collateralized by government securities. Central banks have also lowered the interest rates charged to member banks (called the discount rate in the U.S.) for short-term loans. Both measures effectively lubricate the financial system, in two key ways. First, they help provide access to funds for those entities with illiquid mortgage-backed securities. This helps these entities avoid selling the MBS at a steep loss. Second, the available funds stimulate the commercial paper market and general economic activity. Specific responses by central banks are included in the subprime crisis impact timeline.

In November 2008, the Fed announced a $600 billion program to purchase the MBS of the GSE, to help lower mortgage rates.

Broad-based programs

Term Auction Facility (TAF)

The Fed is using the Term Auction Facility to provide short-term loans (liquidity) to banks. The Fed increased the monthly amount of these auctions to $100 billion during March 2008, up from $60 billion in prior months. In addition, term repurchase agreements expected to cumulate to $100 billion were announced, which enhance the ability of financial institutions to sell mortgage-backed and other debt. The Fed indicated that both the TAF and repurchase agreement amounts will continue and be increased as necessary. During March 2008, the Fed also expanded the types of institutions to which it lends money and the types of collateral it accepts for loans.

Dollar Swap Lines

Dollar Swap Lines exchanged dollars with foreign central banks for foreign currency to help address disruptions in dollar funding markets abroad.

Term Securities Lending Facility (TSLF)

The Term Securities Lending Facility auctioned loans of U.S. Treasury securities to primary dealers against eligible collateral.

Primary Dealer Credit Facility (PDCF)

Concurrent to the collapse of Bear Stearns, the Fed announced the creation of a new lending facility, the Primary Dealer Credit Facility. The PDCF provided overnight cash loans to primary dealers against eligible collateral.

Asset-Backed Commercial Paper Money Market Mutual Fund Liquidity Facility (AMLF or ABCP MMMF)

The Asset-Backed Commercial Paper Money Market Mutual Fund Liquidity Facility provided loans to depository institutions and their affiliates to finance purchases of eligible asset-backed commercial paper from money market mutual funds.

Commercial Paper Funding Facility (CPFF)

On October 7, 2008 the Federal Reserve further expanded the collateral it will loan against, to include commercial paper. The action made the Fed a crucial source of credit for non-financial businesses in addition to commercial banks and investment firms. Fed officials said they'll buy as much of the debt as necessary to get the market functioning again. They refused to say how much that might be, but they noted that around $1.3 trillion worth of commercial paper would qualify. There was $1. 61 trillion in outstanding commercial paper, seasonally adjusted, on the market as of October 1, 2008, according to the most recent data from the Fed. That was down from $1.70 trillion in the previous week. Since the summer of 2007, the market has shrunk from more than $2.2 trillion.

The Commercial Paper Funding Facility provided loans to a special purpose vehicle to finance purchases of new issues of asset-backed commercial paper and unsecured commercial paper from eligible issuers.

Term Asset-Backed Securities Loan Facility (TALF)

The Term Asset-Backed Securities Loan Facility provided loans to eligible investors to finance purchases of eligible asset-backed securities.

In November 2008, the Fed announced the $200 billion TALF. This program supported the issuance of asset-backed securities (ABS) collateralized by loans related to autos, credit cards, education, and small businesses. This step was taken to offset liquidity concerns.

In March 2009, the Fed announced that it was expanding the scope of the TALF program to allow loans against additional types of collateral.

Assistance to Individual Institutions

Bear Stearns Companies, Inc. acquisition by JP Morgan Chase & Co. (JPMC)

In March 2008, the Fed provided funds and guarantees to enable bank J.P. Morgan Chase to purchase Bear Stearns, a large financial institution with substantial mortgage-backed securities (MBS) investments that had recently plunged in value. This action was taken in part to avoid a potential fire sale of nearly U.S. $210 billion of Bear Stearns' MBS and other assets, which could have caused further devaluation in similar securities across the banking system. In addition, Bear had taken on a significant role in the financial system via credit derivatives, essentially insuring against (or speculating regarding) mortgage and other debt defaults. The risk to its ability to perform its role as a counterparty in these derivative arrangements was another major threat to the banking system.

Programs included a **Bridge Loan**, an overnight loan provided to JPMC subsidiary, with which this subsidiary made a direct loan to Bear Stearns Companies, Inc, and **Maiden Lane (I)**, a special purpose vehicle created to purchase approximately $30 billion of Bear Stearns's mortgage-related assets.

AIG Assistance

The Federal Reserve created five programs to give assistance to AIG:

Revolving Credit Facility, a revolving loan for the general corporate purposes of AIG and its subsidiaries, and to pay obligations as they came due.

Securities Borrowing Facility, which provided collateralized cash loans to reduce pressure on AIG to liquidate residential mortgage-backed securities (RMBS) in its securities lending portfolio.

Maiden Lane II, a special purpose vehicle created to purchase RMBS from securities lending portfolios of AIG subsidiaries.

Maiden Lane III, a special purpose vehicle created to purchase collateralized debt obligations on which AIG Financial Products had written credit default swaps.

Life Insurance Securitization, which was authorized to provide credit to AIG that would be repaid with cash flows from its life insurance businesses. It was never used.

Loans to affiliates of some primary dealers

The Federal Reserve provided loans to broker-dealer affiliates of four primary dealers on terms similar to those for PDCF.

Citigroup Inc. lending commitment

The Citigroup Inc. lending commitment was a commitment to provide non-recourse loan to Citigroup against ringfence assets if losses on asset pool reached $56.2 billion.

Bank of America Corporation lending commitment

The Bank of America Corporation lending commitment was a commitment to provide non-recourse loan facility to Bank of America if losses on ring fence assets exceeded $18 billion (agreement never finalized).

Source http://en.wikipedia.org/wiki/Federal_Reserve_responses_to_the_subprime_crisis

History of Federal Open Market Committee actions

This is a list of historical rate actions by the United States **Federal Open Market Committee** (FOMC). The FOMC controls the supply of credit to banks and the sale of treasury securities. At scheduled meetings, the FOMC meets and makes any changes it sees as necessary, notably to the federal funds rate and the discount rate. The committee may also take actions with a less firm target, such as an increasing liquidity by the sale of a set amount of Treasury bonds, or affecting the price of currencies both foreign and domestic by selling dollar reserves (such as during the Mexican peso bailout in 1994).

Famous actions

Operation Twist (1961)

The Federal Open Market Committee action known as **Operation Twist** (named for the Twist dance craze of the time) began in 1961. The intent was to flatten the yield curve in order to promote capital inflows and strengthen the dollar. The Fed utilized open market operations to shorten the maturity of public debt in the open market. It performs the 'twist' by selling some of the short term debt (with three years or less to maturity) it purchased as part of the quantitative easing policy back into the market and using the money received from this to buy longer term government debt. Although this action was marginally successful in reducing the spread between long-term maturities and short-term maturities, Vincent Reinhart and others have suggested it did not continue for a sufficient period of time to be effective. Despite being considered a failure since a 1966 near-term analysis by Franco Modigliani and Richard Sutch, the action has subsequently been reexamined and in a 2011 paper economist Eric Swanson of the Federal Reserve Bank of San Francisco has suggested that "Operation Twist" was more effective than originally thought. Swanson suggested similar action as an alternative to quantitative easing by central banks; the FOMC did in fact take an analogous action in 2011.

Saturday Night Special (1979)

Soon after becoming chairman, Paul Volcker's federal reserve increased the Fed Funds rate from 11% to 12% during the weekend (October 6, 1979).

Quantitative Easing 1 (QE1, December 2008 to March 2010)

"On November 25, 2008, the Federal Reserve announced that it would purchase up to $600 billion in agency mortgage-backed securities (MBS) and agency debt. On December 1, Chairman Bernanke provided further details in a speech. On December 16, the program was formally launched by the FOMC. On March 18, 2009, the FOMC announced that the program would be expanded by an additional $750 billion in purchases of agency MBS and agency debt and $300 billion in purchases of Treasury securities.

Quantitative Easing 2 (QE2, November 2010 to June 2011)

On November 3, 2010, the Fed announced that it would purchase $600 billion of longer dated treasuries, at a rate of $75 billion per month. That program, popularly known as "QE2", concluded in June 2011.

Operation Twist (2011)

The Federal Open Market Committee concluded its September 21, 2011 Meeting at about 2:15 p.m. EDT by announcing the implementation of Operation Twist. This is a plan to purchase $400 billion of bonds with maturities of 6 to 30 years and to sell bonds with maturities less than 3 years, thereby extending the average maturity of the Fed's own portfolio. This is an attempt to do what Quantitative Easing (QE) tries to do, without printing more money and without expanding the Fed's balance sheet, therefore hopefully avoiding the inflationary pressure associated with QE. This announcement brought a bout of risk aversion in the equity markets and strengthened the US Dollar, whereas QE I had weakened the USD and supported the equity markets. Further, on June 20, 2012 the Federal Open Market Committee announced an extension to the Twist programme by adding additionally $267 billion thereby extending it throughout 2012.

Quantitative easing 3 (QE3)

On September 13, 2012, the Federal Reserve announced a third round of quantitative easing (QE3). This new round of quantitative easing provided for an open-ended commitment to purchase $40 billion agency mortgage-backed securities per month until the labor market improves "substantially". Some economists believe that Scott Sumner's blog on nominal income targeting played a role in popularizing the "wonky, once-eccentric policy" of "unlimited QE".

Quantitative easing 4 (QE4)

The Federal Open Market Committee voted to order a fourth round of quantitative easing (QE4) on December 12, 2012. This round authorized up to $40 billion worth of agency mortgage-backed securities per month, and $45 billion worth of longer-term Treasury securities.

Historical actions

Currently, this only shows meetings, both scheduled and unscheduled "emergency" meetings. The FOMC makes a number of other important pronouncements as well such as during testimony to Congress whose effects are harder to quantify.

Red dates are intermeeting actions. Blue signifies tightening, green signifies neutrality, and yellow signifies easing.

Date	Fed. Fund Rate	Discount Rate	Votes	Note
Jun 22, 2011	0.00–0.25%	0.75%	X-X	Offi State
Dec 16, 2008	0.00–0.25%	0.50%	10–0	Offi State See a ZIRI
Oct 29, 2008	1.00%	1.25%	10–0	Offi State
Oct 8, 2008	1.50%	1.75%	X–X	This emer unsc meet resp rapic weal econ mad coor with othe bank the v Offi State
Apr 30, 2008	2.00%	2.25%	8–2	The cut r 25 b poin drew their bias som remo "dov risks grow rema its st but l sign futu to th rate Fish Plos disse prefe chan Offi State
Mar 18, 2008	2.25%	2.50%	8–2	The mad unus large slash basis off t fede rate resp turm mark the c of B Stea Desp pred even 100 poin mark rallie resp Fish Plos disse prefe smal Offi State
Mar 16, 2008	3.00%	3.25%	10–0	This emer unsc meet resp the r at B Stea FOM arran secu JPM Chas grea buyo Bear to m certa Bear wou back also for t creat fund safe secu less ones bank lastl the diffe betw disc and fede rate basis to 25 Offi State
January 30, 2008	3.00%	3.50%	9–1	Fish disse prefe chan Offi State
January 22, 2008	3.50%	4.00%	8–1	This inter rate in re to th Janu dow with resul annc Tues morn befo S. m open Pool

				disse sayi emer actic not r and wait sche meet Misl abse Offi State
Dec 11, 2007	4. 25%	4.75%	9–1	Rose disse prefe 50 b. poin The disa with basis cut, resp Fed state day (Dec 12) an ir mon supp mark conj with centi Offi State 2007 Offi State 2007
Oct 31, 2007	4. 50%	5.00%	9–1	Hoe disse prefe chan Offi State
Sep 18, 2007	4. 75%	5.25%	10–0	Offi State
Aug 17, 2007	5. 25%	5.75%	10–0	The subp mort crisi the r shor the F Aug meet caus boar relea state Aug sayi they prep act i resp the c and I incre liqui an unsc meet Aug the F "tem redu sprea betw prim cred and fede rate basis from poin estab Janu Offi State 2007 Offi State 2007 Offi State 2007
Aug 7, 2007	5. 25%	6.25%	10–0	Offi State
Jun 28, 2007	5. 25%	6.25%	10–0	Offi State
May 9, 2007	5. 25%	6.25%	10–0	Offi State
Mar 21, 2007	5. 25%	6.25%	10–0	Bies hers Offi State
January 31, 2007	5. 25%	6.25%	11–0	Offi State
Dec 12, 2006	5. 25%	6.25%	10–1	Lack disse prefe 25 b. poin incre Offi State
Oct 25, 2006	5. 25%	6.25%	10–1	Lack disse prefe 25 b. poin incre Offi State
Sep 20, 2006	5. 25%	6.25%	10–1	Lack disse prefe 25 b. poin incre Offi State
Aug 8, 2006	5. 25%	6.25%	9–1	The rates this they raise rates basis for s cons meet prior disse prefe 25 b. poin incre Offi State
Jun 29, 2006	5. 25%	6.25%	10–0	Offi State
May 10, 2006	5. 00%	6.00%	10–0	Offi State
Mar 28, 2006	4. 75%	5.75%	11–0	This Bern first as ne Chai repla Alan Gree He c Gree polic grad tight and incre trans for tl Fede Rese Offi State
January 31, 2006	4. 50%	5.50%	10–0	Offi State
Dec 13, 2005	4. 25%	5.25%	10–0	Offi State

November 1, 2005	4.00%	5.00%	10–0	Offi State
September 20, 2005	3.75%	4.75%	9–1	Olso disse prefe chan Offi State
Aug 9, 2005	3.50%	4.50%	9–1	Offi State
Jun 30, 2005	3.25%	4.25%	11–0	Offi State
May 3, 2005	3.00%	4.00%	10–0	Offi State
Mar 22, 2005	2.75%	3.75%	11–0	Offi State
Feb 2, 2005	2.50%	3.50%	12–0	Offi State
Dec 14, 2004	2.25%	3.25%	12–0	The chan prev polic relea mint each Prev the r were only next had finis rend them histo inter was to be relea three after of a decis mint beca avail pred the F actic next Offi State
Nov 10, 2004	2.00%	3.00%	12–0	Offi State
Sep 21, 2004	1.75%	2.75%	12–0	Offi State
Aug 10, 2004	1.50%	2.50%	12–0	Offi State
Jun 30, 2004	1.25%	2.25%	12–0	Offi State
May 4, 2004	1.00%	2.00%	12–0	Offi State
Mar 16, 2004	1.00%	2.00%	12–0	Offi State
January 28, 2004	1.00%	2.00%	12–0	Offi State
Dec 9, 2003	1.00%	2.00%	12–0	Offi State
Oct 28, 2003	1.00%	2.00%	12–0	Offi State
Sep 16, 2003	1.00%	2.00%	12–0	Offi State
Aug 12, 2003	1.00%	2.00%	12–0	Offi State
Jun 25, 2003	1.00%	2.00%	11–1	Parr disse prefe 50 b poin Offi State
May 6, 2003	1.25%	2.25%	12–0	Offi State
Mar 18, 2003	1.25%	2.25%	12–0	Offi State
January 29, 2003	1.25%	2.25%	12–0	Offi State
January 9, 2003	1.25%	2.25%		No r but r disc winc intro Octc impl Thes mani disc 100 poin than fede rate, effec hikir 150 poin Offi State
Dec 10, 2002	1.25%	0.75%	12–0	Offi State

Source http://en.wikipedia.org/wiki/History_of_Federal_Open_Market_Committee_actions

History of the Federal Reserve System

Federal Reserve Board, 1917

This article is about the history of the United States Federal Reserve System from its creation to the present.

Central banking in the United States prior to the Federal Reserve

The Federal Reserve System is the third central banking system in the United States' history. The First Bank of the United States (1791–1811) and the Second Bank of the United States (1817–1836) each had 20-year charters, and both issued currency, made commercial loans, accepted deposits, purchased securities, had multiple branches, and acted as fiscal agents for the U.S. Treasury. In both banks the Federal Government was required to purchase 20% of the bank's capital stock and appoint 20% of the directors. Thus majority control was in the hands of private investors who purchased the rest of the stock. The banks were opposed by state-chartered banks, who saw them as very large competitors, and by many who understood them to be banking cartels which compelled to them servitude of the common man. President Andrew Jackson vetoed legislation to renew the Second Bank of the United States, starting a period of free banking. Jackson staked his second term on the issue of central banking stating, "Every monopoly and all exclusive privileges are granted at the expense of the public, which ought to receive a fair equivalent. The many millions which this act proposes to bestow on the stockholders of the existing bank must come directly or indirectly out of the earnings of the American people."

In 1863, as a means to help finance the Civil War, a system of national banks was instituted by the National Currency Act. The banks each had the power to issue standardized national bank notes based on United States bonds held by the bank. The Act was totally revised in 1864 and later named as the National-Bank Act, or National Banking Act, as it is popularly known. The administration of the new national banking system was vested in the newly created Office of the Comptroller of the Currency and its chief administrator, the Comptroller of the Currency. The Office, which still exists today, examines and supervises all banks chartered nationally and is a part of the U.S. Treasury Department.

The Federal Reserve Act

National bank currency was considered inelastic because it was based on the fluctuating value of U.S. Treasury bonds rather than the growing desire for easy credit. If Treasury bond prices declined, a national bank had to reduce the amount of currency it had in circulation by either refusing to make new loans or by calling in loans it had made already. The related liquidity problem was largely caused by an immobile, pyramidal reserve system, in which nationally chartered country banks were required to set aside their reserves in reserve city banks, which in turn were required to have reserves in central city banks. During planting season country banks needed to call in their reserves, and during the harvest season they would add to their reserves. A national bank whose reserves were being drained would replace its reserves by selling stocks and bonds, by borrowing from a clearing house or by calling in loans. As there was little in the way of deposit insurance, if a bank was rumored to be having liquidity problems then this might cause many people to remove their funds from the bank. Because of the crescendo effect of banks which lent more than their assets could cover, during the last quarter of the 19th century and the beginning of the 20th century, the United States economy went through a series of financial panics.

The National Monetary Commission

A particularly severe panic in 1907 provided the motivation for renewed demands for banking and currency reform. The following year Congress enacted the Aldrich-Vreeland Act which provided for an emergency currency and established the National Monetary Commission to study banking and currency reform.

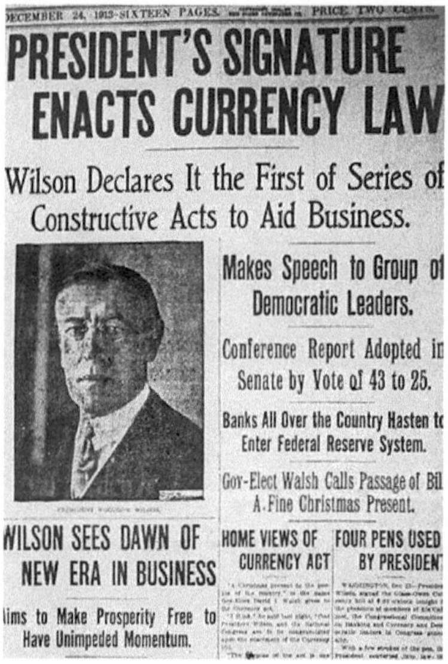
ECEMBER 24, 1913—SIXTEEN PAGES. PRICE TWO CENTS

PRESIDENT'S SIGNATURE ENACTS CURRENCY LAW

Wilson Declares It the First of Series of Constructive Acts to Aid Business.

Makes Speech to Group of Democratic Leaders.

Conference Report Adopted in Senate by Vote of 43 to 25.

Banks All Over the Country Hasten to Enter Federal Reserve System.

Gov-Elect Walsh Calls Passage of Bill A Fine Christmas Present.

WILSON SEES DAWN OF NEW ERA IN BUSINESS

ims to Make Prosperity Free to Have Unimpeded Momentum.

HOME VIEWS OF CURRENCY ACT

FOUR PENS USED BY PRESIDENT

The chief of the bipartisan National Monetary Commission was financial expert and Senate Republican leader Nelson Aldrich. Aldrich set up two commissions — one to study the American monetary system in depth and the other, headed by Aldrich, to study the European central-banking systems and report on them.

Aldrich went to Europe opposed to centralized banking but, after viewing Germany's banking system, he came away believing that a centralized bank was better than the government-issued bond system that he had previously supported. Centralized banking was met with much opposition from politicians, who were suspicious of a central bank and who charged that Aldrich was biased due to his close ties to wealthy bankers such as J.P. Morgan and his daughter's marriage to John D. Rockefeller, Jr.

In 1910, Aldrich and executives representing the banks of J.P. Morgan, Rockefeller, and Kuhn, Loeb & Co., secluded themselves for ten days at Jekyll Island, Georgia. The executives included Frank A. Vanderlip, president of the National City Bank of New York, associated with the Rockefellers; Henry Davison, senior partner of J.P. Morgan Company; Charles D. Norton, president of the First National Bank of New York; and Col. Edward House, who would later become President Woodrow Wilson's closest adviser and founder of the Council on Foreign Relations. There, Paul Warburg of Kuhn, Loeb, & Co. directed the proceedings and wrote the primary features of what would be called the Aldrich Plan. Warburg would later write that "The matter of a uniform discount rate (interest rate) was discussed and settled at Jekyll Island." Vanderlip wrote in his 1935 autobiography *From Farmboy to Financier*:

Despite my views about the value to society of greater publicity for the affairs of corporations, there was an occasion, near the close of 1910, when I was as secretive, indeed, as furtive as any conspirator. None of us who participated felt that we were conspirators; on the contrary we felt we were engaged in a patriotic work. We were trying to plan a mechanism that would correct the weaknesses of our banking system as revealed under the strains and pressures of the panic of 1907. I do not feel it is any exaggeration to speak of our secret expedition to Jekyl Island as the occasion of the actual conception of what eventually became the Federal Reserve System. ... Discovery, we knew, simply must not happen, or else all our time and effort would be wasted. If it were to be exposed publicly that our particular group had gotten together and written a banking bill, that bill would have no chance whatever of passage by Congress. Yet, who was there in Congress who might have drafted a sound piece of legislation dealing with the purely banking problem with which we were concerned?

Despite meeting in secret, from both the public and the government, the importance of the Jekyll Island meeting was revealed three years after the Federal Reserve Act was passed, when journalist Bertie Charles Forbes in 1916 wrote an article about the "hunting trip".

The 1911-12 Republican plan was proposed by Aldrich to solve the banking dilemma, a goal which was supported by the American Bankers' Association. The plan provided for one great central bank, the National Reserve Association, with a capital of at least $100 million and with 15 branches in various sections. The branches were to be controlled by the member banks on a basis of their capitalization. The National Reserve Association would issue currency, based on gold and commercial paper, that would be the liability of the bank and not of the government. The Association would also carry a portion of member banks' reserves, determine discount reserves, buy and sell on the open market, and hold the deposits of the federal government. The branches and businessmen of each of the 15 districts would elect thirty out of the 39 members of the board of directors of the National Reserve Association.

Aldrich fought for a private monopoly with little government influence, but conceded that the government should be represented on the board of directors. Aldrich then presented what was commonly called the "Aldrich Plan"—which called for establishment of a "National Reserve Association"—to the National Monetary Commission. Most Republicans and Wall Street bankers favored the Aldrich Plan, but it lacked enough support in the bipartisan Congress to pass.

Because the bill was introduced by Aldrich, who was considered the epitome of the "Eastern establishment," the bill received little support. It was derided by southerners and westerners who believed that wealthy families and large corporations ran the country and would thus run the proposed National Reserve Association. The National Board of Trade appointed Warburg as head of a committee to persuade Americans to support the plan. The committee set up offices in the then-45 states and distributed printed materials about the proposed central bank. The Nebraskan populist and frequent Democratic presidential candidate William Jennings Bryan said of the plan: "Big financiers are back of the Aldrich currency scheme." He asserted that if it passed, big bankers would "then be in complete control of everything through the control of our national finances."

There was also Republican opposition to the Aldrich Plan. Republican Sen. Robert M. LaFollette and Rep. Charles Lindbergh Sr. both spoke out against the favoritism that they contended the bill granted to Wall Street. "The Aldrich Plan is the Wall Street Plan...I have alleged that there is a 'Money Trust'", said Lindbergh. "The Aldrich plan is a scheme plainly in the interest of the Trust". In response, Rep. Arsène Pujo, a Democrat from Oklahoma, obtained congressional authorization to form and chair a subcommittee (the Pujo Committee) within the House Committee Banking Committee, to conduct investigative hearings on the alleged "Money Trust." The hearings continued for a full year and were led by the Subcommittee's counsel, Democratic lawyer Samuel Untermyer, who later also assisted in drafting the Federal Reserve Act. The "Pujo hearings" convinced much of the populace that America's money largely rested in the hands of a select few on Wall Street. The Subcommittee issued a report saying:

"If by a 'money trust' is meant an established and well-defined identity and community of interest between a few leaders of finance...which has resulted in a vast and growing concentration of control of money and credit in the hands of a comparatively few men...the condition thus described exists in this country today...To us the peril is manifest.. .When we find...the same man a director in a half dozen or more banks and trust companies all located in the same section of the same city, doing the same class of business and with a like set of associates similarly situated all belonging to the same group and representing the same class of interests, all further pretense of competition is useless.... "

Seen as a "Money Trust" plan, the Aldrich Plan was opposed by the Democratic Party as was stated in its 1912 campaign platform, but the platform also supported a revision of banking laws intended to protect the public from financial panics and "the domination of what is known as the "Money Trust." During the 1912 election, the Democractic Party took control of the Presidency and both chambers of Congress. The newly elected president, Woodrow Wilson, was committed to banking and currency reform, but it took a great deal of his political influence to get an acceptable plan passed as the Federal Reserve Act in 1913. Wilson thought the Aldrich plan was perhaps "60-70% correct". When Virginia Rep. Carter Glass, chairman of the House Committee on Banking and Currency, presented his bill to President-elect Wilson, Wilson said that the plan must be amended to contain a Federal Reserve Board appointed by the executive branch to maintain control over the bankers.

After Wilson presented the bill to Congress, a group of Democratic congressmen revolted. The group, led by Representative Robert Henry of Texas, demanded that the "Money Trust" be destroyed before it could undertake major currency reforms. The opponents particularly objected to the idea of regional banks having to operate without the implicit government protections that large, so-called money-center banks would enjoy. The group almost succeeded in killing the bill, but were mollified by Wilson's promises to propose antitrust legislation after the bill had passed, and by Bryan's support of the bill.

The enactment of the Federal Reserve Act

After months of hearings, amendments, and debates the Federal Reserve Act passed Congress in December, 1913. The bill passed the House by an overwhelming majority of 298 to 60 on December 22, 1913 and passed the Senate the next day by a vote of 43 to 25. An earlier version of the bill had passed the Senate 54 to 34, but almost 30 senators had left for Christmas vacation by the time the final bill came to a vote. Most every Democrat was in support of and most Republicans were against it. As noted in a paper by the American Institute of Economic Research:

In its final form, the Federal Reserve Act represented a compromise among three political groups. Most Republicans (and the Wall Street bankers) favored the Aldrich Plan that came out of Jekyll Island. Progressive Democrats demanded a reserve system and currency supply owned and controlled by the Government in order to counter the "money trust" and destroy the existing concentration of credit resources in Wall Street. Conservative Democrats proposed a decentralized reserve system, owned and controlled privately but free of Wall Street domination. No group got exactly what it wanted. But the Aldrich plan more nearly represented the compromise position between the two Democrat extremes, and it was closest to the final legislation passed.

Frank Vanderlip, one of the Jekyll Island attendees and the president of National City Bank, wrote in his autobiography:

Although the Aldrich Federal Reserve Plan was defeated when it bore the name Aldrich, nevertheless its essential points were all contained in the plan that was finally adopted.

Ironically, in October 1913, two months before the enactment of the Federal Reserve Act, Frank Vanderlip proposed before the Senate Banking Committee his own competing plan to the Federal Reserve System, one with a single central bank controlled by the Federal government, which almost derailed the legislation then being considered and already passed by the U.S. House of Representatives. Even Aldrich stated strong opposition to the currency plan passed by the House.

However, the former point was also made by Republican Representative Charles Lindbergh Sr. of Minnesota, one of the most vocal opponents of the bill, who on the day the House agreed to the Federal Reserve Act told his colleagues:

"But the Federal reserve board have no power whatever to regulate the rates of interest that bankers may charge borrowers of money. This is the Aldrich bill in disguise, the difference being that by this bill the Government issues the money, whereas by the Aldrich bill the issue was controlled by the banks...Wall Street will control the money as easily through this bill as they have heretofore. "(Congressional Record, v. 51, page 1447, Dec. 22, 1913)

Republican Congressman Victor Murdock of Kansas, who voted for the bill, told Congress on that same day:

"I do not blind myself to the fact that this measure will not be effectual as a remedy for a great national evil – the concentrated control of credit...The Money Trust has not passed [died]... You rejected the specific remedies of the Pujo committee, chief among them, the prohibition of interlocking directorates. He [your enemy] will not cease fighting...at some half-baked enactment...You struck a weak half-blow, and time will show that you have lost. You could have struck a full blow and you would have won."

In order to get the Federal Reserve Act passed, Wilson needed the support of populist William Jennings Bryan, who was credited with ensuring Wilson's nomination by dramatically throwing his support Wilson's way at the 1912 Democratic convention. Wilson appointed Bryan as his Secretary of State. Bryan served as leader of the agrarian wing of the party and had argued for unlimited coinage of silver in his "Cross of Gold Speech" at the 1896 Democratic convention. Bryan and the agrarians wanted a government-owned central bank which could print paper money whenever Congress wanted, and thought the plan gave bankers too much power to print the government's currency. Wilson sought the advice of prominent lawyer Louis Brandeis to make the plan more amenable to the agrarian wing of the party; Brandeis agreed with Bryan. Wilson convinced them that because Federal Reserve notes were obligations of the government and because the president would appoint the members of the Federal Reserve Board, the plan fit their demands. However, Bryan soon became disillusioned with the system. In the November 1923 issue of *"Hearst's Magazine"* Bryan wrote that "The Federal Reserve Bank that should have been the farmer's greatest protection has become his greatest foe."

Southerners and westerners learned from Wilson that the system was decentralized into 12 districts and surely would weaken New York and strengthen the hinterlands. Sen. Robert L. Owen of Oklahoma eventually relented to speak in favor of the bill, arguing that the nation's currency was already under too much control by New York elites, whom he alleged had singlehandedly conspired to cause the 1907 Panic.

Large bankers thought the legislation gave the government too much control over markets and private business dealings. The *New York Times* called the Act the "Oklahoma idea, the Nebraska idea"—referring to Owen and Bryan's involvement.

However, several Congressmen, including Owen, Lindbergh, LaFollette, and Murdock claimed that the New York bankers feigned their disapproval of the bill in hopes of inducing Congress to pass it. The day before the bill was passed, Murdock told Congress:

"You allowed the special interests by pretended dissatisfaction with the measure to bring about a sham battle, and the sham battle was for the purpose of diverting you people from the real remedy, and they diverted you. The Wall Street bluff has worked."

When Wilson signed the Federal Reserve Act on December 23, 1913, he said he felt grateful for having had a part "in completing a work ... of lasting benefit for the country," knowing that it took a great deal of compromise and expenditure of his own political capital to get it enacted. This was in keeping with the general plan of action he made in his First Inaugural Address on March 4,

1913, in which he stated:

We shall deal with our economic system as it is and as it may be modified, not as it might be if we had a clean sheet of paper to write upon; and step-by-step we shall make it what it should be, in the spirit of those who question their own wisdom and seek counsel and knowledge, not shallow self-satisfaction or the excitement of excursions we can not tell.

While a system of 12 regional banks was designed so as not to give eastern bankers too much influence over the new bank, in practice, the Federal Reserve Bank of New York became "first among equals". The New York Fed, for example, is solely responsible for conducting open market operations, at the direction of the Federal Open Market Committee. Democratic Congressman Carter Glass sponsored and wrote the eventual legislation, and his home state capital of Richmond, Virginia, was made a district headquarters. Democratic Senator James A. Reed of Missouri obtained two districts for his state. However, the 1914 report of the Federal Reserve Organization Committee, which clearly laid out the rationale for their decisions on establishing Reserve Bank districts in 1914, showed that it was based almost entirely upon current correspondent banking relationships. To quell Elihu Root's objections to possible inflation, the passed bill included provisions that the bank must hold at least 40% of its outstanding loans in gold. (In later years, to stimulate short-term economic activity, Congress would amend the act to allow more discretion in the amount of gold that must be redeemed by the Bank.) Critics of the time (later joined by economist Milton Friedman) suggested that Glass's legislation was almost entirely based on the Aldrich Plan that had been derided as giving too much power to elite bankers. Glass denied copying Aldrich's plan. In 1922, he told Congress, "no greater misconception was ever projected in this Senate Chamber."

Wilson named Warburg and other prominent experts to direct the new system, which began operations in 1915 and played a major role in financing the Allied and American war efforts. Warburg at first refused the appointment, citing America's opposition to a "Wall Street man", but when World War I broke out he accepted. He was the only appointee asked to appear before the Senate, whose members questioned him about his interests in the central bank and his ties to Kuhn, Loeb, & Co.'s "money trusts".

Accord of 1951 between the Federal Reserve and the Treasury Department

Post Bretton-Woods era

In July 1979, Paul Volcker was nominated, by President Carter, as Chairman of the Federal Reserve Board amid roaring inflation. He tightened the money supply, and by 1986 inflation had fallen sharply. In October 1979 the Federal Reserve announced a policy of "targeting" money aggregates and bank reserves in its struggle with double-digit inflation.

In January 1987, with retail inflation at only 1%, the Federal Reserve announced it was no longer going to use money-supply aggregates, such as M2, as guidelines for controlling inflation, even though this method had been in use from 1979, apparently with great success. Before 1980, interest rates were used as guidelines; inflation was severe. The Fed complained that the aggregates were confusing. Volcker was chairman until August 1987, whereupon Alan Greenspan assumed the mantle, seven months after monetary aggregate policy had changed.

2001 Recession to Present

From early 2001 to mid 2003 the Federal Reserve lowered its interest rates 13 times, from 6.25 to 1.00%, to fight recession. In November 2002, rates were cut to 1.75, and many interest rates went below the inflation rate. On June 25, 2003, the federal funds rate was lowered to 1.00%, its lowest nominal rate since July, 1958, when the overnight rate averaged 0.68%. Starting at the end of June 2004, the Federal Reserve System raised the target interest rate and then continued to do so 17 straight times.

In March 2006, the Federal Reserve ceased to make public M3, because the costs of collecting this data outweighed the benefits. M3 includes all of M2 (which includes M1) plus large-denomination ($100,000 +) time deposits, balances in institutional money funds, repurchase liabilities issued by depository institutions, and Eurodollars held by U. S. residents at foreign branches of U.S. banks as well as at all banks in the United Kingdom and Canada.

2008 subprime mortgage crisis

Due to a credit crunch caused by the sub-prime mortgage crisis in September 2007, the Federal Reserve began cutting the federal funds rate. The Fed cut rates by 0.25% after its December 11, 2007 meeting and disappointed many individual investors who expected a higher rate cut: the Dow Jones Industrial Average dropped by nearly 300 points at its close that day. The Fed slashed the rate 0.75% in an emergency action on January 22, 2008 to assist in reversing a significant market slide influenced by weakening international markets. The Dow Jones Industrial Average initially fell nearly 4% (465 points) at the start of trading and then rebounded to a more tolerable 1.06% (128 point) loss. On January 30, 2008, eight days after the 75 points decrease, the Fed lowered its rate again, this time by 50 points.

Key laws affecting the Federal Reserve

Key laws affecting the Federal Reserve have been:

Banking Act of 1935
Employment Act of 1946
Federal Reserve-Treasury Department Accord of 1951
Bank Holding Company Act of 1956 and the amendments of 1970
Federal Reserve Reform Act of 1977
International Banking Act of 1978
Full Employment and Balanced Growth Act (1978)
Depository Institutions Deregulation and Monetary Control Act (1980)
Financial Institutions Reform, Recovery and Enforcement Act of 1989

Federal Deposit Insurance Corporation Improvement Act of 1991
Gramm-Leach-Bliley Act (1999)
Source http://en.wikipedia.org/wiki/History_of_the_Federal_Reserve_System

Jekyll Island

Jekyll Island	
Location	Glynn County, Georgia, USA
Nearest city	Brunswick, Georgia
Coordinates	31°4′12″N 81°25′13″W
Established	October 7, 1947
Governing body	Jekyll Island Authority

Jekyll Island is an island off the coast of the U.S. state of Georgia, in Glynn County; it is one of the Sea Islands and one of the Golden Isles of Georgia. The city of Brunswick, Georgia, the Marshes of Glynn, and several other islands, including the larger St. Simons Island, are nearby. Its beaches are frequented by vacationers and guided tours of the Landmark Historic District are available. Bike trails, walks along the beaches and sandbars, and Summer Waves, a water park are a few of the many things vacationers can do. The historic district consists of a number of buildings from the late nineteenth and early twentieth centuries. The island is also full of wildlife, consisting of many different mammals, reptiles, and birds living and breeding in the island's inland marshes.

Physical setting

Jekyll Island is one of only four Georgia barrier islands that feature a paved causeway to access the island by car. It features 5,700 acres (23 km) of land, including 4,400 acres (18 km) of solid earth and a 200-acre (0.81 km) Jekyll Island Club Historic District. The rest is tidal marshlands, mostly on the island's western shore. The island measures about 7 miles (11 km) long by 1.5 miles (2.4 km) wide, has 8 miles (13 km) of wide, flat beaches on its east shore with sand packed hard enough for easy walking or biking, and boasts 20 miles (32 km) of hiking trails.

Like the other Golden Isles, Jekyll is mostly made of older Pleistocene land mass and smaller sections of younger Holocene land.

Northern end of the Island

The north end of the island is the main area that has been impacted by human development over the past few hundred years. Early settlers and the loggers that came after they developed plantations in this area and made fallen trees to be used for extra-strong ships during wartime. In later years, much of this wilderness has been developed into golf courses.

Clam Creek Picnic Area

A short winding road leads to a parking lot and one of the three picnic areas on the island. To the west is a vast marsh hammock and an astounding view of the Sidney Lanier Bridge, a 480-foot (150 m) tall cable stay bridge on Hwy 17. There is a large fishing pier that extends northwest from the picnic area. To the east, a bridge crosses Clam Creek in front of an inland marsh to connect the picnic area to the North End Beach and Driftwood Beach. These beaches are characterized by another tidal creek emptying into St. Simons Sound and a boneyard of pine and live oak tree roots.

Horton House

The Horton House ruins in 2007

A two-story structure built from tabby in 1742 stands in ruins along N. Riverview Rd. The house was occupied by Major William Horton during the British colonial period, who also brewed beer in Georgia's first brewery (the ruins of which are a few hundred yards down the road). This structure has been meticulously preserved over the past 100 years as an example of coastal Georgia building techniques and as one of the oldest surviving buildings in the state. Across the street from the Horton House ruins is the du Bignon cemetery, a tabby wall surrounding the graves of five people who all died in the 19th century.

Campground

Just across the street from the entrance to the Clam Creek picnic area is the campground, an 18-acre (73,000 m) facility in a cleared maritime forest. The campground has running water for restrooms, showers, and laundry, as well as a store and bike rentals.

Southern end

The southern end of the island was virtually unused by settlers and visitors until the 20th century. The multiple parallel dunes on the southernmost tip are a result of the eroding north beaches traveling southward and being deposited in a recurved spit.

South Dunes picnic area

This picnic area on the ocean side of the island features plenty of picnic tables, a full bathroom with showers and a boardwalk to traverse the 20-foot (6.1 m) high dune ridge that protects this wooded area from sea breezes. This area was repaired in 1983, with bulldozers pushing new primary dunes into place to correct the damage caused by 30 years of beachgoers trampling over the enormous dunes to the beach.

Glory Beach

Access to this beach is by way of a long boardwalk built in the mid-1980s by the producers of the film *Glory*, and it can be accessed from the soccer complex at the north end of the Jekyll Island 4-H center property. The boardwalk passes through a variety of natural habitats ranging from ancient dunes to freshwater sloughs.

St. Andrews picnic area

The farthest point on the beach from Clam Creek, St. Andrews is a picnic area on the river side of the island, facing the marsh and mainland. This beach is very popular with fishing birds and dolphins, surfacing for air, can commonly be seen to the south of the north.

In 2008, the Jekyll Island History Museum, the Jekyll Island Authority, and the Friends of Historic Jekyll Island commemorated the survivors of the slave ship Wanderer, the last slavery vessel to transport slaves without repercussions. On November 28 of 1858, nearly 50 years after the legal importing of slaves was outlawed in the United States, The Wanderer anchored near the southern portion of Jekyll Island, transporting 465 enslaved Africans ashore. The historic site includes 12-foot (3. 7 m) tall steel sculptures of ship sails, signifying the cold hard reality of slavery.

Jekyll Island Club Historic District

Jekyll Island Club Hotel

In the midsection of the river side of the island is a 240-acre (0.97 km) Historic District where most of the buildings from the Jekyll Island Club era still stand, most in remarkable preservation. The centerpiece of the grounds is the enormous Jekyll Island Club Hotel, a two-winged structure that contains numerous suites for rental, including a beautiful presidential suite that contains the three-story turret on the front of the building. Thirty-three buildings from the late nineteenth and early twentieth centuries surround the hotel, with many being mansion-sized cottages. Rooms in some of these cottages are for rent, while others exist as museums, art galleries, or bookstores. The hotel is listed in the National Register of Historic Places. The historic district itself has been listed as a National Historic Landmark District since 1978.

Tram tours originate from the Jekyll Island Museum located on Stable Rd. directly across from the historic district several times daily and detail much of the history of this area.

History

Native American settlement

In the mid-2nd millennium, the island now known as Jekyll was part of a coastal Georgia Native American chiefdom called Guale. Muskogian tribes, who comprised a majority of the Creek Nation, were the inhabitants of this territory.

The surrounding creeks yielded fish that were speared easily by hunters, and the tribes utilized native vegetation for food and drink, gathering nuts and fruit, even making a type of tea from parched holly leaves. These settlers also allegedly grew pumpkins, beans, tobacco, sunflowers, and corn among other crops.

Arrival of Europeans

Explorers from Spain were the first to make an official claim to Jekyll Island in 1510, giving it the name *Isla De Ballenas* (Whale Island) and later Juan Ponce de Leon served as the civil governor of this and Spain's other claimed North American territories. In 1562 French explorer Jean Ribault claimed the island for France and renamed the island *Ille de la Somme*. Ribault later surrendered to the Spanish and was executed, an event that began a conflict between the two countries along the Georgia and Florida coasts. After his army swiftly defeated the French, Philip II of Spain immediately had a colony established on Jekyll.

More brief conflicts between these two countries along the coastline followed, and Spanish priests had established missions with the intention of converting Native Americans to Christianity. Upset that their culture, including dances, banquets, and bonfires, was being suppressed, natives from the modern area of Darien began destroying the missions and slaying the priests in a southward journey; however, Father Davilla on Jekyll was spared, and kept as a slave (though he was later released to the Spanish in a prisoner exchange).

In 1663–65, England established grants to land stretching southward from their Jamestown colony to an area below St. Augustine, Florida. The English allied themselves with the Cherokee, Creek, and Yuchi tribes, and sent members of these tribes armed with English weapons to attack the Spanish and Native American settlements on Jekyll in 1681–83. By 1702, the English had driven the Spanish from the entire area.

The English occupation

Major William Horton's tabby-structure home. Built in 1742, this image was taken in 1927.

General James Oglethorpe established Georgia as a colony in 1733. Jekyll Island was named shortly thereafter by Oglethorpe in honor of his friend, Sir Joseph Jekyll, For many years, including the "Club Era", it was misspelled as Jekyl Island. The additional "L" was later re-added by the Georgia legislature in 1929 to correctly spell the name of the former sponsor of the colony. Prior to English settlement along the coast of Georgia, the Spanish had established missions in the coastal Georgia area. No mission is known to have been established on Jekyll; however, the Spanish influenced the island from the mission that was established on St. Simons Island before the English settlement.

In the late 1730s, General Oglethorpe appointed William Horton to set up a military post in the area to protect Fort Frederica on St Simon's Island. By 1738 Horton had set up permanent residence on Jekyll Island, near what is now called DuBignon Creek. At his residence, Horton established a plantation prosperous enough to supply the population at Frederica with beef and corn.

Driftwood Beach on Jekyll Island

Horton continued to make improvements on Jekyll throughout his years on the island. Even after his property was destroyed in 1742 during Spanish attacks, he rebuilt his home and worked on new experimental crops on his plantation, including barley and indigo. Horton's wood residence was soon burned and ravaged by the Spanish, forcing him to rebuild his home and plantation after the Spanish attacks with the uniquely native material, Tabby. A mixture of lime, oyster shell and water, this strong building material withstood the test of time and the external structure of William Horton's home is now one of two remaining two-story colonial-era structures in the state of Georgia. William Horton died in 1748–1749 and his property on Jekyll passed through many hands until, just before the year 1800, the entire island became the property of Christophe du Bignon.

Plantation era

Christophe du Bignon and his family arrived here in 1792. The family came to the United States in order to escape the French Revolution, which devastated provincial families like the du Bignons. The plantation that du Bignon owned on Jekyll was very prosperous. Christophe du Bignon also introduced

Inland marshes of Jekyll Island

slavery to the island. Christophe died in 1825 and ownership passed on to his son Henri Charles Du Bignon. Under the new ownership of Henri Charles the plantation continued to prosper, as evidenced by the 1850 census.

On November 28, 1858, fifty years after the importation of slaves to the United States was made illegal, the ship The Wanderer landed on Jekyll Island with 465 slaves. This was the next-to-last successful shipment of slaves to American soil from Africa.

However, by 1860, there was a great decline in the productivity on Jekyll. By 1862 when Union Army troops arrived, the Du Bignon plantation was completely deserted. After the American Civil War ended, the Du Bignon family returned to the island. Henri Charles divided the island up among his four children.

In the late 1870s John Eugene Du Bignon became owner of property on the island. He had bought the southern third of the island from his uncle's estate, intending to establish a home there.

The Jekyll Island Club

duBignon Cottage

Du Bignon, who had inherited the southern third of the island from his father, purchased the rest of the island

Rockefeller Cottage

from his siblings with the help of his brother-in-law Newton Finney and an investor. Their plan to sell the island as a winter retreat for the wealthy came to fruition on February 17, 1886, and the clubhouse was completed in January 1888. Fifty-three members purchased shares for $600 each, and a limit of 100 members was imposed to preserve the club's exclusivity.

From 1888 to 1942 the club opened every January, except a few because of yellow fever outbreaks, to accommodate some of the world's wealthiest people. Members and their families enjoyed activities such as biking, hunting, horseback riding, and tennis, and frequented the north beaches. Some of the more esteemed members built mansion-sized cottages that still stand in excellent condition today. During the Great Depression the club experienced financial difficulties, and by the time the United States entered World War II the era of the Jekyll Island Club was over. The State of Georgia bought the island in 1947.

Planning of the Federal Reserve System

At the end of November 1910, Senator Nelson W. Aldrich and Assistant Secretary of the U.S. Treasury Department A. Piatt Andrew, and five of the country's leading financiers (Frank Vanderlip, Henry P. Davison, Charles D. Norton, Benjamin Strong, and Paul Warburg) arrived at the Jekyll Island Club to discuss monetary policy and the banking system, an event that led to the creation of the current, privately owned Federal Reserve. According to the Federal Reserve Bank of Atlanta, the 1910 Jekyll Island meeting resulted in draft legislation for the creation of a U.S. central bank. Parts of this draft (the Aldrich plan) were incorporated into the 1913 Federal Reserve Act. On November 5–6, 2010, Ben Bernanke stayed on Jekyll Island to commemorate the 100-year anniversary of this original meeting. The Conference was the first official confirmation of the revelations made initially in 1949 by *Ezra Pound* to *Eustace Mullins* in his work *Secrets of The Federal Reserve* and later reported by *G. Edward Griffin* in his book The Creature from Jekyll Island.

Forbes magazine founder Bertie Charles Forbes wrote several years later:

Picture a party of the nation's greatest bankers stealing out of New York on a private railroad car under cover of darkness, stealthily riding hundred[s] of miles South, embarking on a mysterious launch, sneaking onto an island deserted by all but a few servants, living there a full week under such rigid secrecy that the names of not one of them was once mentioned, lest the servants learn the identity and disclose to the world this strangest, most secret expedition in the history of American finance. I am not romancing; I am giving to the world, for the first time, the real story of how the famous Aldrich currency report, the foundation of our new currency system, was written... The utmost secrecy was enjoined upon all. The public must not glean a hint of what was to be done. Senator Aldrich notified each one to go quietly into a private car of which the railroad had received orders to draw up on an unfrequented platform. Off the party set. New York's ubiquitous reporters had been foiled... Nelson (Aldrich) had confided to Henry, Frank, Paul, and Piatt that he was to keep them locked up at Jekyll Island, out of the rest of the world, until they had evolved and compiled a scientific currency system for the United States, the real birth of the present Federal Reserve System, the plan done on Jekyll Island in the conference with Paul, Frank, and Henry... Warburg is the link that binds the Aldrich system and the present system together. He more than any one man has made the system possible as a working reality.

Development of the Jekyll Island Authority

Initially, Jekyll Island was part of the State Park system. However, by 1950, as costs associated with getting the island ready for visitation began to mount, the island was taken out of the state park system and organized into a separate authority in order to become self-sustaining.

The Jekyll Island Authority was created in February 1950 under the direction of Governor Herman Talmadge, and was designed to be a governing board. This board consisted of nine gubernatorial appointed members and was charged with the operation and care of the island.

The authority placed a convict camp on the island in 1951, and the prisoners readied the island for public use, executing landscaping for drainage and for the foundations of motels and neighborhoods and building the perimeter road. From September 1951 to December 1954, the island was primarily closed to the public. Upon completion of the six-year causeway project and drawbridge erection on December 11, 1954, Jekyll Island officially re-opened to the public.

Because the post-WWII plan for Jekyll was for the island to become self-sufficient, and because the Authority was receiving negative publicity in the mid-1950s, the Georgia Legislature restructured the Authority in 1957. Board members became elected officials and included the attorney general, state auditor, public service commissioner, state parks department director, and secretary of state.

In the decade following this restructuring motels, houses, the convention center, and a shopping center were constructed, as well as the towers at the entrance to the causeway. In the 1970s the Authority began renovating the cottages and club hotel in the historic district, and the 1980s saw construction of bike paths and the re-opening of the clubhouse in December 1987. Two more reorganizations of the Authority in the 1970s and 1980s changed the board to consist of the commissioner of the Georgia Department of Natural Resources and eight citizens of the state.

Some of the later advancements made by the Jekyll Island Authority include the Soccer Complex, the Jekyll Island Tennis Center, a Historic District registered with National Historic Landmark Status in 1978, Jekyll Island 4-H Center opened in 1983 to connect children to the island's ecosystem and most recently, the Georgia Sea Turtle Center.

In 2006, plans to revitalize the island were put into place after years of significantly declining visitation numbers. In 2007 the Jekyll Island Authority selected Linger Longer Communities LLC to be its private partner in redeveloping a portion of the Island. After a year of planning and hosting public forums throughout the state of Georgia, the Authority and Linger Longer developed a revitalization plan that included a renovated Convention Center and mixed-use public Beach Village to occupy a very similar footprint to that of the current Convention Center, beach deck, and adjacent asphalt parking lot. The Beach Village is also set to include an area for new retail shops as well as a public beach-side promenade.

A once-per-day toll has been charged for several decades to enter Jekyll Island. The rate was one dollar in 1985, but has increased since then and became five dollars in August 2009, and later to 6 dollars.

By legislative mandate, sixty five percent of the island is and will remain in a mostly natural state (including parks and picnic areas).

Use as a filming location

Scenes from the films *X-Men: First Class*, *Glory*, *The Legend Of Bagger Vance*, *Jekyll Island*, and *The View From Pompey's Head* were filmed on Jekyll Island.

Research and further reading

Bagwell, Tyler (1999). *The Jekyll Island Club*. Arcadia.

Condominium Hotel & Conference Center, Jekyll Island, GA see www.jekyllislandga.com

Jekyll Island Photo and Information

Booklet Jekyll Island Museum & Jekyll Island Authority
McCash, June Hall. *Jekyll Island's Early Years*. University of Georgia Press. 2005. ISBN 0-8203-2447-7.
McCash, June Hall. The Jekyll Island Cottage Colony. University of Georgia Press. 1998. ISBN 0-8203-1928-7.
McCash, William Barton and June Hall McCash. The Jekyll Island Club: Southern Haven for America's Millionaires. University of Georgia Press. 1989. ISBN 0-8203-1070-0
The Jekyll Island Museum and archives, Jekyll Island, Georgia
Wilkins, Thomas Hart (Summer 2007, XCI,2). "Sir Joseph Jekyll and his Impact on Oglethorpe's Georgia". Georgia Historical Quarterly. pp. 119–134.
Source http://en.wikipedia.org/wiki/Jekyll_Island

Paul Warburg

Paul Warburg

Paul Warburg

Born	August 10, 1868 Hamburg, Germany
Died	January 24, 1932 (aged 63) New York City, U.S.
Nationality	United States
Occupation	Banker, International Business
Employer	Manhattan Company

Paul Moritz Warburg (August 10, 1868 – January 24, 1932) was a German-born American banker and early advocate of the U.S. Federal Reserve System.

Early life

Warburg was born in Hamburg, Germany, to the Warburg banking family. His parents were Moritz and Charlotte (Esther) Warburg. After graduating from the Realgymnasium in Hamburg in 1886, he entered the employ of Simon Hauer, a Hamburg importer and exporter, to learn the fundamentals of business practice. He similarly worked for Samuel Montague & Company, bankers, in London in 1889–90, the Banque Russe pour le Commerce Etranger in Paris in 1890–91.

In 1891, Warburg entered the office of the family banking firm of M. M. Warburg & Co., which had been founded in 1798 by his great-grandfather. He interrupted work there to undertake a world tour during the winter of 1891–92. Warburg was admitted to a partnership in the family firm in 1895.

On October 1, 1895, Warburg was married in New York City to Nina J. Loeb, daughter of Solomon Loeb, founder of the New York investment firm of Kuhn, Loeb & Co. The Warburgs were the parents of a son, James Paul Warburg, and a daughter, Bettina Warburg.

Career

Although a major factor in German finance, after frequent business trips to New York Warburg settled there in 1902 as a partner in Kuhn, Loeb & Co. , where the influential Jacob Schiff, his wife's brother-in-law, was senior partner. Warburg remained a partner in the family firm in Hamburg, but he became a naturalized American citizen in 1911. He was a member of Temple Emanu-El in New York City.

Warburg was elected a director of Wells Fargo & Company in February 1910. He resigned in September 1914 following his appointment to the Federal Reserve Board, and Jacob Schiff was elected to his seat on the Wells Fargo board.

Warburg became known as a persuasive advocate of central banking in America. Many of his contemporaries regarded him as the chief driving force behind the establishment of America's central bank. Russell Leffingwell, who served variously as the Assistant Secretary of the Treasury, head of the Council on Foreign Relations, and chairman of J.P. Morgan credited Warburg with doing "yeoman's service in preaching the doctrines and practices of modern [central] European banking" while all other "friends of sound money" were so occupied with battling against the free silver movement that they gave scant thought to the need for currency reform. Father Coughlin's periodical, Social Justice, saw Warburg's influence on the final form of the Federal Reserve Act's as on a par with that of the bill's main sponsor, Congressman Carter Glass, charging them both with the "chief credit for 'putting over' the Federal Reserve System." Harold Kellock of The Century Magazine went even further, characterizing Warburg as "the mildest-mannered man that ever personally conducted a revolution." This shy and sensitive man, Kellock continued, "imposed his idea on a nation of a hundred million people."

Upon arriving in New York in 1902, Warburg drafted a critique of the American banking system, which he thought was insufficiently centralized. Self-conscious of his imperfect English and his status as a newcomer, however, he left his paper to sit in his desk for four years. He overcame his reticence in 1906 after attending a dinner party hosted by Professor Edwin Seligman of Columbia University. Seligman, an advocate of central banking, was impressed with Warburg's extensive knowledge of the financial system and reportedly told him that "It's your duty to get your ideas before the country."

Shortly thereafter, The New York Times published Warburg's "Defects and Needs of our Banking System." Concerning its financial system, he argued, "The United States is in fact at about the same point that had been reached by Europe at the time of the Medicis, and by Asia, in all likelihood, at the time of Hammurabi." The chief reason for this lagging state of development was the lack of a central institution that could rediscount bank promissory notes to facilitate the exchange of promises of future payment for cash. A central bank constructed along the lines of the Reichsbank could fulfill this role, according to Warburg, and thus make it easier for the excess reserves of one bank to be used to bolster the insufficient reserves of another.

Warburg's ideas gained a wider hearing after the panic of 1907 engulfed the country's financial system, and he subsequently published two more articles elaborating and defending his plans, "A Plan for a Modified Central Bank" and "A United Reserve Bank of the United States." At the same time, he appeared at conferences hosted by Columbia University, the American Economic Society, and the Academy of Political Science.

By 1908, Warburg had gained enough recognition that Nelson Aldrich, the prominent Republican senator from Rhode Island, consulted him for advice on currency reform. The National Monetary Commission, which Aldrich chaired, subsequently interviewed Warburg on multiple occasions. In 1910, Aldrich invited Warburg to attend a secretive meeting with other influential bankers on Jekyll Island in Georgia, where the draft of a bill to establish a central bank was worked out. This bill was close enough to the outline that he adumbrated in his three articles that Harold Kellock could write, "Five years from the time Mr. Warburg had begun his single-handed crusade, his ideas were place before Congress in the form of the Aldrich Bill."

The Aldrich Bill, however, did not become the Federal Reserve Act. The Owen-Glass Bill did. But modern scholars such as Elmus Wicker, Murray Rothbard, and William Greider believe that the Aldrich and Owen-Glass bills are so similar that there is little doubt the latter plan was heavily influenced by the former. "The New York bankers got all they wanted," Wicker argues, "with the single exception of banker control....The Federal Reserve Act owes as much, if not more, to Senator Aldrich as it does to Representative Glass." Despite some minor quibbles, Warburg himself largely celebrated the Owen-Glass Bill in The North American Review. It was "a source of great satisfaction," he wrote, that both the Democratic and Republican parties had come to embrace the type of plan for which reformers like him had been campaigning.

In 1919, he founded and became first chairman of the American Acceptance Council. He organized and became the first chairman of the International Acceptance Bank of New York in 1921. International Acceptance was acquired by the Bank of the Manhattan Company in 1929, with Warburg becoming chairman of the combined organization.

He became a director of the Council on Foreign Relations at its founding in 1921, remaining on the board until his death. From 1921 to 1926 Warburg was a member of the advisory council of Federal Reserve Board, serving as president of the advisory council in 1924–26. He was also a trustee of the Institute of Economics, founded in 1922; when it was merged into the Brookings Institution in 1927, he became a trustee of the latter, serving until his death.

Warburg was notable for his March 8, 1929, warning of the disaster threatened by the wild stock speculation then rampant in the United States, foretelling the crash which occurred in October of that year.

He encouraged German–American cultural cooperation, helping found the Carl Schurz Memorial Foundation in 1930 and serving as its treasurer from May 1930 until his death. He also made substantial contributions to the Warburg Library in Hamburg, founded by his family; gave to Heidelberg University one of its halls, known as the American House; and he made generous donations to the Academy of Political Science in Berlin.

Death

Warburg died at his home in New York City on January 24, 1932, and was buried in Sleepy Hollow Cemetery in Sleepy Hollow, New York. At the time of his death he was chairman of the Manhattan Company and a director of the Bank of Manhattan Trust Company, Farmers Loan and Trust Company of New York, First National Bank of Boston, Baltimore & Ohio Railroad, Union Pacific Railroad, Los Angeles & Salt Lake Railroad, Western Union Telegraph Company, American I.G. Chemical Company, Agfa Ansco Corporation, and Warburg & Company of Amsterdam.

Legacy

The cartoon character, Oliver "Daddy" Warbucks in the *Little Orphan Annie* series, was purportedly inspired by Warburg's life and times. The Paul M. Warburg chair in Economics at Harvard University was named in his honor.

Family

His son James Warburg (1896–1969) was a financial adviser to Franklin D. Roosevelt in the first years of his presidency.

Source http://en.wikipedia.org/wiki/Paul_Warburg

Too big to fail

The **"too big to fail"** theory asserts that certain financial institutions are so large and so interconnected that their failure would be disastrous to the economy, and they therefore must be supported by government when they face difficulty. The colloquial term "too big to fail" was popularized by U.S. Congressman Stewart McKinney in a 1984 Congressional hearing, discussing the Federal Deposit Insurance Corporation's intervention with Continental Illinois. The term had previously been used occasionally in the press.

Proponents of this theory believe that some institutions are so important that they should become recipients of beneficial financial and economic policies from governments or central banks. Some economists such as Paul Krugman hold that economies of scale in banks and in other businesses are worth preserving, so long as they are well regulated in proportion to their economic clout, and therefore that "too big to fail" status can be acceptable. The global economic system must also deal with sovereign states being too big to fail.

Opponents believe that one of the problems that arises is moral hazard whereby a company that benefits from these protective policies will seek to profit by it, deliberately taking positions (see Asset allocation) that are high-risk high-return, as they are able to leverage these risks based on the policy preference they receive. The term has emerged as prominent in public discourse since the 2007–2010 global financial crisis. Critics see the policy as counterproductive and that large banks or other institutions should be left to fail if their risk management is not effective. Some critics, such as Alan Greenspan, believe that such large organisations should be deliberately broken up: "If they're too big to fail, they're too big". More than fifty prominent economists, financial experts, bankers, finance industry groups, and banks themselves have called for breaking up large banks into smaller institutions.

On March 6, 2013, United States Attorney General Eric Holder told the Senate Judiciary Committee that the Justice Department faces difficulty charging large banks with crimes because of the risk to the economy. Four days later, Federal Reserve Bank of Dallas President Richard W. Fisher wrote in advance of a speech to the Conservative Political Action Conference that large banks should be broken up into smaller banks, and both Federal Deposit Insurance and Federal Reserve discount window access should end for large banks. Other conservatives including Thomas Hoenig, Ed Prescott, Glenn Hubbard, and David Vitter also advocated breaking up the largest banks.

On April 10, 2013, International Monetary Fund Managing Director Christine Lagarde told the Economic Club of New York "too big to fail" banks had become "more dangerous than ever" and needed to be controlled with "comprehensive and clear regulation [and] more intensive and intrusive supervision."

Regulatory basis

Before 1950, U.S. federal bank regulators had essentially two options for resolving an insolvent institution: closure, with liquidation of assets and payouts for insured depositors, or purchase and assumption, encouraging the acquisition of assets and assumption of liabilities by another firm. A third option was made available by the Federal Deposit Insurance Act of 1950: providing assistance, the power to support an institution through loans or direct federal acquisition of assets, until it could recover from its distress.

The statute limited the "assistance" option to cases where "continued operation of the bank is essential to provide adequate banking service." Regulators shunned this third option for many years, fearing that if regionally or nationally important banks were thought to be generally immune to liquidation, markets in their shares would be distorted. Thus, the assistance option was never employed during the period 1950-1969, and very seldom thereafter. Research into historical banking trends suggests that the consumption loss associated with National Banking Era bank runs was far more costly than the consumption loss from stock market crashes.

Continental Illinois case

Distress

The Continental Illinois National Bank and Trust Company experienced a fall in its overall asset quality during the early 1980s. Tight money, Mexico's default (1982) and plunging oil prices followed a period when the bank had aggressively pursued commercial lending business, Latin American syndicated loan business, and loan participations in the energy sector. Complicating matters further, the bank's funding mix was heavily dependent on large certificates of deposit and foreign money markets, which meant its depositors were more risk-averse than average retail depositors in the US.

Payments crisis

The bank held significant participation in highly-speculative oil and gas loans of Oklahoma's Penn Square Bank. When Penn Square failed in July 1982, the Continental's distress became acute, culminating with press rumors of failure and an investor-and-depositor run in early May 1984. In the first week of the run, the Fed permitted the Continental Illinois discount window credits on the order of $3.6 billion. Still in significant distress, the management obtained a further $4.5 billion in credits from a syndicate of money center banks the following week. These measures failed to stop the run, and regulators were confronted with a crisis.

Regulatory crisis

The seventh-largest bank in the nation by deposits would very shortly be unable to meet its obligations. Regulators faced a tough decision about how to resolve the matter. Of the three options available, only two were seriously considered. Even banks much smaller than the Continental were deemed unsuitable for resolution by liquidation, owing to the disruptions this would have inevitably caused. The normal course would be to seek a purchaser (and indeed press accounts that such a search was underway contributed to Continental depositors' fears in 1984). However, in the tight-money financial climate of the early 1980s, no purchaser was forthcoming.

Besides generic concerns of size, contagion of depositor panic and bank distress, regulators feared the significant disruption of national payment and settlement systems. Of special concern was the wide network of correspondent banks with high percentages of their capital invested in the Continental Illinois. Essentially, the bank was deemed "too big to fail," and the "provide assistance" option was reluctantly taken. The dilemma now became, how to provide assistance without significantly unbalancing the nation's banking system?

Stopping the run

To prevent immediate failure, the Federal Reserve announced categorically that it would meet any liquidity needs the Continental might have, while the Federal Deposit Insurance Corporation (FDIC) gave depositors and general creditors a full guarantee (not subject to the $100,000 FDIC deposit-insurance limit) and provided direct assistance of $2 billion (including participations). Money center banks assembled an additional $5.3 billion unsecured facility pending a resolution and resumption of more-normal business. These measures slowed, but did not stop, the outflow of deposits.

Controversy

In a United States Senate hearing afterwards, the then Comptroller of the Currency C. T. Conover defended his position by admitting the regulators will not let the largest 11 banks fail. Regulatory agencies (FDIC, Office of the Comptroller of the Currency, the Federal Reserve System, etc.) feared that such failures could cause widespread financial

A man at Occupy Wall Street protesting institutions deemed too big to fail.

complications and a major bank run that might easily spread by financial contagion. The implicit guarantee of too-big-to-fail has been criticized by many, including the president of the Federal Reserve Bank of Dallas Richard Fisher, for its preferential treatment of large banks.

Simultaneously, the perception of too-big-to-fail may diminish healthy market discipline, and may have influenced the decisions behind the insolvency of Washington Mutual in 2008. For example, large depositors in banks not covered by the policy tend to have a strong incentive to monitor the bank's financial condition, and/or withdraw in case the bank's policies exposes them to high risks, since FDIC guarantees have an upper limit. However, large depositors in a "too big to fail" bank would have less incentive, since they'd expect to be bailed out in the event of failure.

The Federal Deposit Insurance Corporation Improvement Act was passed in 1991, giving the FDIC the responsibility to rescue an insolvent bank by the least costly method. The Act had the implicit goal of eliminating the widespread belief among depositors that a loss of depositors and bondholders will be prevented for large banks. However, the Act included an exception in cases of systemic risk, subject to the approval of two-thirds of the FDIC Board of Directors, the Federal Reserve Board of Governors, and the Treasury Secretary.

Ron Suskind claimed in his book *Confidence Men* that the administration of Barack Obama considered breaking up Citibank and other large banks that had been involved in the financial crisis of 2008. He said that Obama's staff, such as Timothy Geithner, refused to do so. The administration and Geithner have denied this version of events.

Implicit guarantee subsidy

Since the full amount of the deposits and debts of "too big to fail" banks are effectively guaranteed by the government, large depositors view deposits with these banks as a safer investment than deposits with smaller banks. Therefore, large banks are able to pay lower interest rates to depositors than small banks are obliged to pay.

In October 2009, Sheila Bair, at that time the Chairperson of the FDIC, commented:

"'Too big to fail' has become worse. It's become explicit when it was implicit before. It creates competitive disparities between large and small institutions, because everybody knows small institutions can fail. So it's more expensive for them to raise capital and secure funding."

Research has shown that banking organizations are willing to pay an added premium for mergers that will put them over the asset sizes that are commonly viewed as the thresholds for being too big to fail.

Estimated value

A study conducted by the Center for Economic and Policy Research found that the difference between the cost of funds for banks with more than $100 billion in assets and the cost of funds for smaller banks widened dramatically after the formalization of the "too big to fail" policy in the U.S. in the fourth quarter of 2008. This shift in the large banks' cost of funds was in effect equivalent to an indirect "too big to fail" subsidy of $34 billion per year to the 18 U. S. banks with more than $100 billion in assets.

Another study by Frederic Schweikhard and Zoe Tsesmelidakis, employing Merton Model of pricing corporate debt, estimates the amount saved by America's biggest banks from having a perceived safety net of a government bailout was $120 billion from 2007 to 2010. For America's biggest banks the saving broke down to $53 billion for Citigroup, $32 billion for Bank of America, $10 billion for JPMorgan, $8 billion for Wells Fargo, and $4 billion for AIG. The model employs the Merton Model of pricing corporate debt, and compares the difference in confidence between stockholders and debt holders of the large banks. It noted that passage of the Dodd-Frank Act — which promised an end to bailouts — did nothing to raise the price of credit (i.e., lower the implicit subsidy) for the "too-big-too-fail" institutions.

"Too big to fail is too big"

More than fifty economists, financial experts, bankers, finance industry groups, and banks themselves have called for breaking up large banks into smaller institutions. (See also Divestment.)

Mervyn King, the governor of the Bank of England, called for banks that are "too big to fail" to be cut down to size, as a solution to the problem of banks having taxpayer-funded guarantees for their speculative investment banking activities. "If some banks are thought to be too big to fail, then, in the words of a distinguished American economist, they are too big. It is not sensible to allow large banks to combine high street retail banking with risky investment banking or funding strategies, and then provide an implicit state guarantee against failure."

Alistair Darling disagreed; "Many people talk about how to deal with the big banks – banks so important to the financial system that they cannot be allowed to fail. But the solution is not as simple, as some have suggested, as restricting the size of the banks". As well, Alan Greenspan said that "If they're too big to fail, they're too big," suggesting U.S. regulators to consider breaking up large financial institutions considered "too big to fail." He added, "I don't think merely raising the fees or capital on large institutions or taxing them is enough ... they'll absorb that, they'll work with that, and it's totally inefficient and they'll still be using the savings."

Some critics have argued that "The way things are now banks reap profits if their trades pan out, but taxpayers can be stuck picking up the tab if their big bets sink the company." Additionally, as discussed by Senator Bernie Sanders, if taxpayers are contributing to save these companies from bankruptcy, they "should be rewarded for assuming the risk by sharing in the gains that result from this government bailout."

In this sense, Alan Greenspan affirms that, "Failure is an integral part, a necessary part of a market system." Thereby, although the financial institutions that were bailout were indeed important to the financial system, the fact that they took risk beyond what they would otherwise, should be enough for the Government to let them face the consequences of their actions. It would have been a lesson to motivate institutions to proceed differently next time.

Too big to fail tax

Moreover, the decision to bailout large institutions does not seem a sustainable solution. It does not fix the causes; it addresses the consequences. The interesting point is that authorities have not realized that institutions that were at the center of the crisis, namely JP Morgan Chase, Bank of America, Wells Fargo and Citigroup, have become "even bigger", representing what one Democratic socialist politician, Rep. Bernie Sanders, called "the four largest banks in America." Thereby, the question that the Government should think about is: If one of these banks tends to fail, will we have the capacity to save it? The problem will certainly reach a point where it will be impossible for authorities to handle. Hence, a more sustainable method should be explored as well, such as letting the banks fail, with free market correction as the recovery.

Thus, Willem Buiter proposes a tax to internalize the massive external costs inflicted by "too big to fail" institution. "When size creates externalities, do what you would do with any negative externality: tax it. The other way to limit size is to tax size. This can be done through capital requirements that are progressive in the size of the business (as measured by value added, the size of the balance sheet or some other metric). Such measures for preventing the New Darwinism of the survival of the fittest and the politically best connected should be distinguished from regulatory interventions based on the narrow leverage ratio aimed at regulating risk (regardless of size, except for a de minimis lower limit)."

Financial Stability Board list

On November 4, 2011, a policy research and development entity, called the Financial Stability Board, released a list of 29 banks worldwide that they considered to be "systemically important financial institutions" - financial organisations whose size *and role* meant that any failure could cause serious systemic problems. Of the list, 17 are based in Europe, 8 in the U.S., and 4 in Asia:

- Bank of America
- Bank of China
- Bank of New York Mellon
- Banque Populaire CdE
- Barclays
- BNP Paribas
- Citigroup
- Commerzbank
- Credit Suisse
- Deutsche Bank
- Goldman Sachs Group
- Crédit Agricole
- HSBC
- ING Bank
- JPMorgan Chase
- Lloyds Banking Group
- Mitsubishi UFJ FG
- Mizuho FG
- Morgan Stanley
- Nordea
- Royal Bank of Scotland
- Santander
- Société Générale
- State Street
- Sumitomo Mitsui FG
- UBS
- Unicredit Group
- Wells Fargo

2013 Attorney General Holder and Dallas Fed President Fisher comments

On March 6, 2013, United States Attorney General Eric Holder testified to the Senate Judiciary Committee that the size of large financial institutions has made it difficult for the Justice Department to bring criminal charges when they are suspected of crimes, because such charges can threaten the existence of a bank and therefore their interconnectedness may endanger the national or global economy. "Some of these institutions have become too large,"

Holder told the Committee, "It has an inhibiting impact on our ability to bring resolutions that I think would be more appropriate," contradicting earlier written testimony from a deputy assistant attorney general who defended the Justice Department's "vigorous enforcement against wrongdoing." Holder has financial ties to at least one law firm benefiting from *de facto* immunity to prosecution, and prosecution rates against crimes by large financial institutions are at 20-year lows.

Four days later, Federal Reserve Bank of Dallas President Richard W. Fisher co-authored a *Wall Street Journal* op-ed about the failure of the Dodd–Frank Wall Street Reform and Consumer Protection Act to provide for adequate regulation of large financial institutions. In advance of his March 8th speech to the Conservative Political Action Conference, Fisher proposed requiring breaking up large banks into smaller banks so that they are "too small to save," ending both Federal Deposit Insurance and Federal Reserve discount window access by larger banks, and requiring disclosure of this lack of federal insurance and financial solvency support to their customers. This was the first time such a proposal had been made by a high ranking U.S. banking official or a prominent conservative. Other conservatives including Thomas Hoenig, Ed Prescott, Glenn Hubbard, and David Vitter also advocated breaking up the largest banks, but liberal commentator Matthew Yglesias questioned their motives and the existence of a true bipartisan consensus.

In a January 29, 2013 letter to Holder, Senators Sherrod Brown and Charles Grassley had criticized this Justice Department policy citing "important questions about the Justice Department's prosecutorial philosophy." After receipt of a DoJ response letter, Brown and Grassley issued a statement saying, "The Justice Department's response is aggressively evasive. It does not answer our questions. We want to know how and why the Justice Department has determined that certain financial institutions are 'too big to jail' and that prosecuting those institutions would damage the financial system."

In Canada

In March 2013, the Office of the Superintendent of Financial Institutions announced that Canada's six largest banks, the Bank of Montreal, the Bank of Nova Scotia, the Canadian Imperial Bank of Commerce, National Bank of Canada, Royal Bank of Canada and Toronto-Dominion Bank, are too big to fail. Those six banks accounted for 90% of banking assests in Canada at that time. As well it noted that "the differences among the largest banks are smaller if only domestic assets are considered, and relative importance declines rapidly after the top five banks and after the sixth bank (National)."

In New Zealand

Despite the goverment's assurances, opposition parties and some media commentators in New Zealand say that the largest banks are too big to fail and have an implicit government guarantee.

In United Kingdom

The British Chancellor (finance minister) George Osborne has threatened to break up banks which are too big to fail.

Source http://en.wikipedia.org/wiki/Too_big_to_fail

Walter Wyatt

Walter Wyatt (July 20, 1893 – February 26, 1978) was an American lawyer, who served as the twelfth Reporter of Decisions of the Supreme Court of the United States.

Born in Savannah, Georgia, Wyatt received his LL.B. from the University of Virginia in 1917. During World War I, Wyatt worked as legal adviser to the Selective Service System, the federal agency charged with enforcing the newly implemented military draft. From 1922 to 1946, he was an attorney for the Federal Reserve System, ending his career there as General Counsel of the agency, and from 1936 to 1946, he also served as counsel to a related agency, the Federal Open Market Committee. During this period, Wyatt also authored several books on banking law.

Wyatt was appointed as the Supreme Court's Reporter of Decisions on March 1, 1946, after the post had been vacant for two years following the death of Ernest Knaebel. He retroactively edited the volumes of the *United States Reports* covering those two years, volumes 322 to 325.

Wyatt died in Washington, D.C. in 1978. Much of his official correspondence and personal papers are stored at the Special Collections Library of the University of Virginia at Charlottesville, Virginia and available for research.

Source http://en.wikipedia.org/wiki/Walter_Wyatt